TALES OF PRINCES PAST

A Memoir of an American Family

TALES OF PRINCES PAST

A Family Memoir by

Marjorie Anne Prince

Copyright © 2022 Marjorie Anne Prince
ALL RIGHTS RESERVED
ISBN 978-1-936003-83-9

Cover art and editorial services by Danforth Prince

Tales of Princes Past

Chapter One	Page 9
The New Territory Beyond the Sea	
Chapter Two	Page 13
From Dutch Culture, Religion, and Language to English	
Chapter Three	Page 15
The Prince Sea Captains in Boston and Colonial Unrest	
Chapter Four	Page 19
The Revolutionary War and the Battle of Brooklyn	
Chapter Five	Page 26
Captain Christopher Prince – A Maritime Adventurer	
Chapter Six	Page 28
The Reign of Cruelty and the End of Slavery in New York	
Chapter Seven	Page 30
John Duffield Prince and Gertrude Helen Martense – A Brilliant Marriage and a Successful Business	
Chapter Eight	Page 34
Ellen Babcock Prince – A Woman of Independent Means and Her Generous Brother William	
Chapter Nine	Page 39
William Babcock Prince – Industrialist and Man About Town	
Chapter Ten	Page 42
Edward Mitchell Prince – Well Mannered Only Son of an Only Son	
Chapter Eleven	Page 48
Full Circle – Back to New York City and Brooklyn	
Author's Biography	Page 54

Front Cover Art

Painting of the farmhouse of Johannes and Hannah De Bevoise by Esther Vanderbilt, wife of Jacob Van Brunt circa 1840.

A miniature portrait in a gold locket frame of a young Captain Christopher Prince circa 1800.

Large portrait of Gertrude Helen Martense Prince circa 1845.

Photograph of Ned Prince and his father Will Prince taken in Cleveland, Ohio in the early 1920's.

Detail from a child's crochet sampler from 1804: ***Lord Grant me Wisdom to Direct my Ways; I ask not Riches nor Yet Length of Days.***

Back Cover Art

William Babcock Prince (left) and his father Jacob Van Brunt Prince (far right) on the porch at their farm in South Coventry, Connecticut. Gentleman in the middle is a close family friend or relative, possibly Will's uncle, William Augustus Babcock.

Helen Christie Prince on her wedding day, April 26, 1913.

The 12th generation of Princes at the wedding of Elizabeth Ann Prince: Rachel Helen Wolff Farley, Jordan Danforth Wolff, Elizabeth Ann Prince Camerlin, Colin Hillyard Barry, and Meghan Elizabeth Barry.

This Book Is Dedicated to the 13th Generation of Princes:

Zoe Rose Farley

James Brendan Farley Jr

Brandon Edward Camerlin

Ryan Eugene Camerlin

August Kamas Barry

"It is only with the heart that one can see rightly. What is essential is invisible to the eye."
Antoine de Saint-Exupéry, pilot, anti-Nazi resistance fighter, and author of *The Little Prince*

Forward

In the very early times *in this country when "The Settlers" were so harassed by the Indians, a lady with her husband, a grown son, and a little babe lived on a farm with no near neighbors. Each morning when the gentlemen went to the fields, they told her if she had any alarms, to blow the horn, a long tin one used to call them to meals. About the middle of the morning, she discovered Indians lurking about, so going to the door, she blew the horn. Her husband and son made great haste to her rescue, but just as they entered the yard, the savages rushed upon them and killed both, then ordered her to go with them. Imagine her agony of mind and apprehension.*

She took her little one in her arms and endeavored to keep pace with them as best she could, but her distress and weakness was so great, she could not; she would fall fainting on the road. They saw the hindrance the child was, then took it by the feet and dashing it against a tree, killed it. Still, they urged her on. Endeavoring to obey, she would sink unconscious again. They would take her by her beautiful long black hair, dip her up and down in a creek and lay her upon the bank until she revived. So, the weary march went on until camp was reached.

Somewhere in the vicinity was an English gentleman and his wife. They heard about her imprisonment and negotiated with the Indians for a sum of money to release her. They then took her to England and later, perhaps several years, returned her to America where she met Mr. Galbraith and married him. They had a daughter, Nancy Galbraith, who married Judge Joseph Edmiston. These were your great grandfather and great grandmother ... (1)

Early drawing of Colonial women being abducted by Native American Warriors. In early American history, captured women and children were often held for ransom; sometimes they became slaves, and sometimes they were adopted by the tribe.

When I was young, my father told me stories from our family's past, some were shocking, some were remarkable. The true story about "The Lady Who Was Captured by Warriors" happened long ago and her name has been forgotten, but "The Lady's" experience at the hands of her captors was terrifying, and I could not imagine how she found the strength and will to survive.

Everyone's family has a past full of interesting and exciting stories. Our family was unique in that we lived in Brooklyn, New York from 1657 – 1920 and we kept paintings, pictures, newspaper articles, and memoirs tucked away in folders and boxes so that there would be a footprint to follow back in time should anyone care to put the pieces together. These records paint a picture of women, men, and children who were courageous, industrious, and self-reliant, who sometimes had an easy path before them and sometimes did not. What our ancestors accomplished during that time was indicative of what hundreds of thousands of families experienced during their first generations in America: they built farms and homesteads, started businesses, fought in wars, lost parents, husbands, wives, and babies, relocated, married, and remarried all the while striving to live a life full of purpose and joy.

I have written a *Tale of Princes Past*, and in so doing, I wish to honor not only those who lived in the past but also those whose families endure to live vibrant and meaningful lives today.

Four Princes in Toledo, Ohio, 1960: Marjie, Ed, Danforth, and Christie

Chapter One

The New Territory Beyond the Sea

There was a New Territory beyond the sea: a land of many rivers, spectacular mountains, and impenetrable forests with no boundaries in sight. Many adventurous people would make this New Land their permanent home.

In 1609 Henry Hudson, an Englishman working for the Dutch, explored the coastline looking for a passage to India. He entered a Great Bay and he saw that the waters swarmed with very large fish and a huge river flowed with the tides north then twelve hours later, south. The natives who lived on the land were clothed in the skins of elk and foxes and their canoes were made from hollow trees. They used bows and arrows with sharp points made of stone. This mainland was called "Mattouwake." Later explorers discovered that the coastline had a Long Island which was separate from the mainland. This Island was called "Sewanhacka" which meant "Island of Shells" because of the enormous quantities of shells that the Native Americans used for currency. In 1624, Fort Amsterdam was built on Manhattan and the foundations were laid for the Dutch city of New Amsterdam.

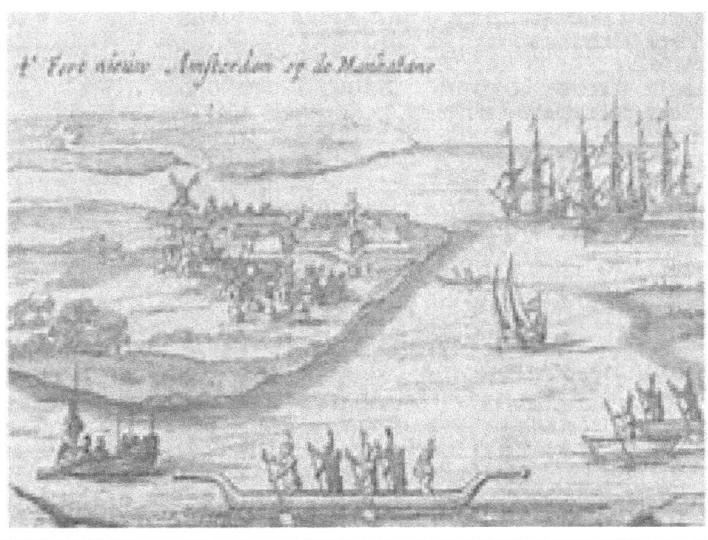

Fort Amsterdam on the southern tip of Manhattan 1624, between the Hudson and the East Rivers. Many Dutch ships and Native Americans in canoes were in the harbor. Notice the windmill and the star shaped fortification.

The voyage across the Atlantic was slow and dangerous, but people in Holland heard about the rich soil and the abundant lands in the New Territory. Many Dutch families made the voyage with all their possessions to make this New World their permanent home. Ships landed in the town of New Amsterdam. Dutch settlers wanted to become farmers, so they looked southward across the river to Sewanhacka, where the land looked like it would be most fertile for

17th Century Dutch Ships brought families and all their possessions from Holland to New Amsterdam.

growing crops. This land had never been plowed or planted and was covered with heavy timber. There were no domestic animals to help clear the land, so the work had to be done entirely by hand using only a hoe and a spade. It was backbreaking work. The first crops that were planted were ones that would yield the most profit from the smallest piece of ground. Tobacco was one crop that was raised successfully and was shipped from New Amsterdam to Holland. Barley was also grown, and vast quantities of malt liquor were made. Soon houses began to spring up along the Sewanhacka shoreline and the first settlement was named "Breuekelen."

The first purchase from the Canarsee Native Americans on Long Island was in 1635 for 'a tract of woodland bounded on the north by the Hills and on the south by the Flatlands and extending east and west in one continual forest.' (2) This tract of land was known as "Flatlands" and the land between Brooklyn and Flatlands was called "Midwout" or Middlewoods. Later the name for this land was simplified and because it was close to "Flatlands" it was called Flatbush.

The Dutch purchased land from the Canarsee Tribe trading black and white seashells, blankets, guns, knives, beer, and brandy.

The sale of all these lands was confirmed in writing by an "Indian Deed" that stated that the Canarsee were the true and original owners, and that they had been paid a fair price. (3) The Dutch settlers made every attempt to respect the rights of the Native Americans, and from their European point of view, no land was taken from the Natives unless it was purchased from the chiefs of the tribes who claimed it. In Native American culture, however, land was never given or sold to anyone in perpetuity. Native Americans gave others the right to share their land for a season or two, in European terms it would be thought of as "rent." These two conflicting ideas of land ownership caused great misunderstanding whenever Europeans and Native Americans transferred land from one group to another.

In 1654 the most southern section of Sewanhacka was settled by several families from Holland who named it New Utrecht. Rutgert Joosten Van Brunt was our first ancestor to move from Holland in 1657 and settle in New Utrecht with his wife Tryntje. On February 17, 1659, another ancestor, Carel De Bevoise emigrated to Brooklyn from Leyden, Holland on the ship **Otter** with his wife, Sophia Van Ladensteyn, and eight-year-old son Jacobus. For the next sixty years, Brooklyn, Flatbush, Flatlands, New Utrecht, and Gravesend became known as the Five Dutch Towns of Kings County.

The first settlement in the town of Flatbush was built along a well-worn Native American path. To concentrate their houses together for the sake of protection against warring Northern Tribes and to create a village of farmers, the first settlers laid out all their farms in narrow oblong shapes fronting both sides of the main road. All subsequent farms were laid out along the same path making the road through town crooked rather than straight. The property on the west side of the road was held almost entirely by three families of Dutch descent: the Lefferts, the Vanderbilts, and the Martense, who were our ancestors.

It was difficult to trace the name of a Dutch ancestor because several hundred years ago the "last name" changed every generation depending on the father's first name. For example, in our family, **Adrian** Reyerze emigrated from Amsterdam in 1646. His son was named Marten **Adrianse** (son of Adrian) and his sons were called "sons of **Marten**" or **Martense**. At this point, in 1725, the family decided to keep the last name Martense, and for the next one hundred years the Martense family were one of the three largest landowners in the village of Flatbush.

In 1654 the area became infested with robbers and pirates, so Brooklyn, Flatbush and Flatlands came together and put a military officer in each town to patrol and protect the people who lived there. Then, in 1670, a Native American leader named Eskemoppas came to the town with his two brothers, Kinnarimas and Ahawaham, and made the claim that they were the true and rightful owners of the land and they wanted to be paid for it. The settlers did not understand this claim since they had in writing the "Indian Deed" from 1635 attesting that the land had been purchased from the Canarsee Tribe. However, it was most important to the Dutch settlers that this matter be settled peacefully.

The Five Dutch Towns of Kings County: Brooklyn, Flatbush, Flatlands, New Utrect, and Gravesend.

A meeting was arranged, and another written agreement was made to give Eskemoppas and his brothers an additional payment for the land. Another document was signed that "gave the land to the Dutch and their heirs and successors forever." (4) The additional payment was as follows:

    10 Fathoms of black seewant wampum (quahaug seashells)
    10 Fathoms or white seewant wampum (periwinkle seashells)
    5 Match Coats of Duffells
    4 Blankets
    2 Gunners sight guns
    2 Pistols
    5 Double handfuls of Powder
    5 Bars of Lead
    10 Knives
    2 Secret aprons of Duffells
    1 Half Barrell of Strong Beer
    3 Cans of Brandy
    6 Shirts

The three Native Americans made their sign on the document, six Dutch witnesses gave their signatures, and the transaction was then approved by the governor.

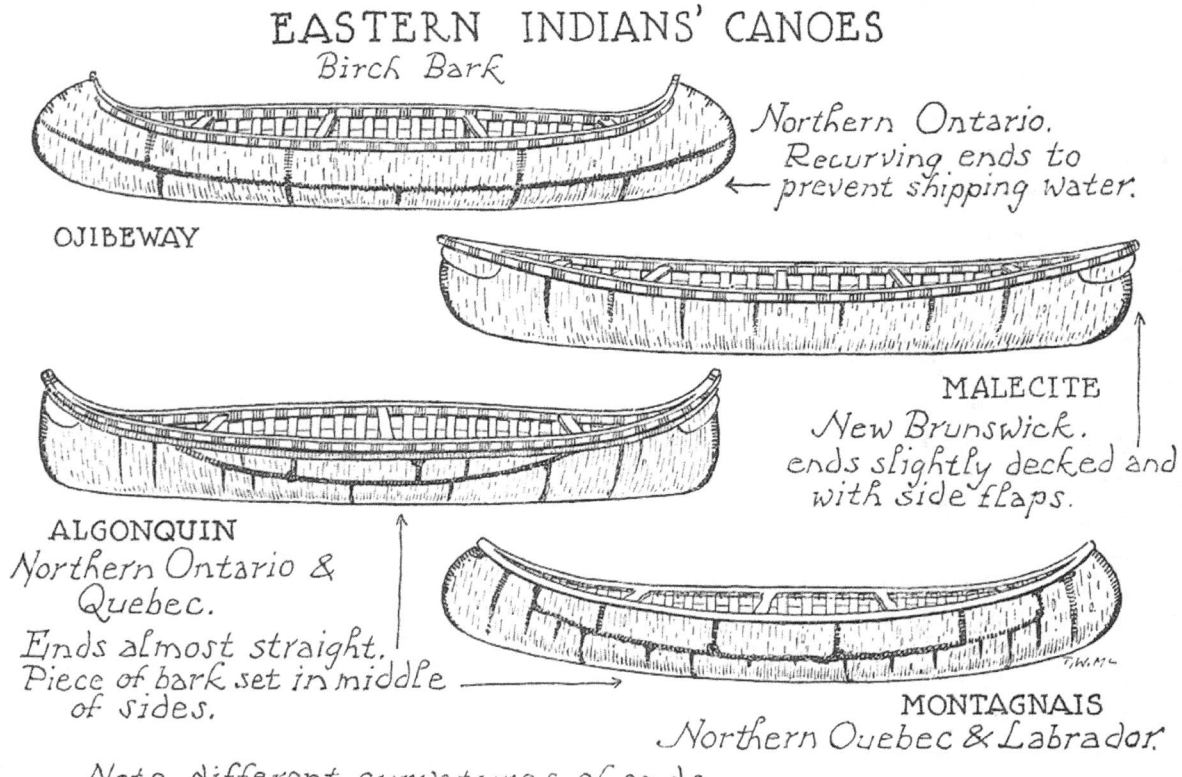

In the 1600's there were 13 Native American tribes living on Long Island, among them were the Canarsee, Shinnecock, Rockaway, Massapequa, Merrick, Setauket, and the Manhasset.

Chapter Two
From Dutch Culture, Religion, and Language to English

The Five Towns of Kings County ("Brooklyn") and Manhattan Island were Dutch in culture, language, and religion but a war in Europe in 1664 changed the lives of these Dutch settlers forever. In 1664, the English won a war against the Dutch in Europe, and this allowed the English to seize all the Dutch counties in North America!

King Charles of England granted Long Island, all the Hudson River, and all lands from the west side of the Connecticut River to the east side of the Delaware Bay to his brother James, the Duke of York. On August 30, three English war ships entered New Amsterdam harbor with fifty guns each and about 450 soldiers. The commander, Col Richard Nicolls, sent a message to the Dutch Governor Peter Stuyvesant demanding immediate surrender. He assured the governor that every Dutch inhabitant would be given his estate, his life, and his liberty if he would submit to the King of England. Governor Stuyvesant wanted to resist the invaders, but the Dutch citizens saw no benefit in fighting against the superior English force. After several days of meetings, a treaty was agreed upon where the Dutch were able to keep their own customs and religion and any Dutch soldier or sailor remaining in the country could stay and receive a portion of farmland or return to Holland as he wished. Col Nicolls was declared governor and the city of New Amsterdam was renamed the city of New York.

The Dutch settlers in New Amsterdam were accustomed to political and religious freedom. Popular education was universal and there was a profound regard for law and order. In 1654 both a church and a school were built in Flatbush and New Amsterdam invited strangers from every race and creed to join its early Colony. The Dutch Government refused to recognize witchcraft or to inflict the death penalty upon those who were suspected of witchcraft by others. They believed in freedom of conscience and equality. They also believed that every citizen should share in local legislation. While they were a Dutch Colony, they had been

Governor Peter Stuyvesant lead his Dutch troops in surrender to the English in 1664. Notice the windmill and the substantial number of British ships in the background.

governed by a "Charter of Liberties," not by a king and they hoped that this form of rule by the citizens would continue. The English, however, were firmly against Dutch self-governance. Soon after they took control, the Duke of York issued a code of laws commonly called the "Duke's Laws." Delegates from the Five Dutch Towns of Kings County came together to review the Laws and make recommendations, but they were told by the British governor that they had no voice in the process of government. The delegates expressed their severe disapproval, but the British court ignored them.

The English made no changes to the Dutch language, schools, or religious practices, so the Dutch "acquiesced" to British rule for the next one hundred years. In all honesty, the Dutch were never content under the rule of the King of England. One hundred years later, the people in New York fought a war of independence from England and the Dutch, as a group, were in favor of this action.

This drawing of The Port of New York in 1679 showed the Stadt Huys (City Hall). Although the city was now under British control, Dutch names and Dutch architecture continued to be used.

Chapter Three

The Prince Sea Captains in Boston and Colonial Unrest

John Prince graduated from Oxford University in England and arrived in Boston in 1633. He worked for two years upon his arrival to pay for his passage, became a freeman in 1635 and married Alice Honor two years later. Family records show that John lived in Cambridge, was an Elder in the Church, and was a respected member of the community. Most men during the Colonial Period in Massachusetts were farmers, but John Prince's youngest son Thomas and grandson Job were part of the ten percent of New Englanders who followed a much more dangerous and exciting path and "took to the sea" and became sea captains. Elder John Prince may have taken some convincing that this was a good career path for his son Thomas, because most New Englanders at that time considered a seafarer's life to be full of sin and vice. Men onboard ship were known to drink and use foul language. Sailors were gone from home for months at a time, and there was always a chance their ship would be lost at sea, and they would never return.

Regardless of the danger, farmers needed sailors onboard ships to take their extra produce, flour, fish, and lumber to the Caribbean. Ships would then return to the Colonies with raw products to be distilled into rum and sugar. Ships would also cross the Atlantic carrying fish to Spain and Portugal in exchange for salt; or they would carry rum to the coast of Africa and return to the Caribbean with slaves to work on the sugar plantations.

A drawing of an 18th Century British Merchant Ship. Prince Sea Captains sailed this type of ship out of Boston Harbor to Europe and the West Indies from 1680 – 1730.

Each year waves of adventure-seeking boys found a place on a merchant or fishing vessel determined to make the sea their calling. If a boy was a good worker on his first few voyages, he might soon be given an officer's berth and he could eventually make a comfortable living. If he found that the sea was not what he expected, he could return to the farm, and he would be replaced by another boy. Thomas was one of the young seafarers who performed well during his first voyages because he rose in the ranks to become Captain Thomas Prince. He sailed his ship ***Dolphin*** for nineteen years to Europe and the West Indies. He was followed by his youngest son, Captain Job Prince who also sailed out of Boston Harbor. Captain Job Prince married Abigail Kimball in 1719 and eleven years later his youngest son Christopher was born.

We do not know what tragedy happened to Job and Abigail, but in April 1734 they both died, leaving their youngest son Christopher aged three, to be raised by family in Boston. Once he became a young man, Christopher Prince worked as a partner in ***Prince Brothers***, his family's trading company. In 1756, at the age of twenty-five, he married Mary Foster and within a year they had their first son Benjamin.

It took a ship five weeks to travel 3,000 miles across the Atlantic Ocean from Boston to London and five weeks to return. King George III of England had never been a soldier and never visited any of this subjects in America, Scotland, or Ireland, yet he demanded that his subjects obey him and all his laws without question. King George decreed that his subjects in the American Colonies pay taxes to support the soldiers he sent to protect them. Many Colonists did not agree with the dictates of a King who was 3,000 miles across the ocean and as early as 1760, hostilities between the King and his Colonists in America grew.

Christopher Prince was a loyal British subject, and he became alarmed at the unrest in Boston between the British soldiers and the Colonists. They were all his close friends and neighbors and people with whom he traded. To avoid taking sides in the growing conflict, Christopher packed up his household and after the birth of his second son John in 1760, he left Boston and sailed north to the British colony of Digby, Nova Scotia. Once in Canada he served as a justice of the peace, a colonel in the militia, and a commissioner of roads. When his first wife died, he married Alice Payson and was later elected to the provincial assembly.

The Boston Massacre March 5, 1770. Nine British soldiers shot into a crowd of protesters killing five and wounding six.

Meanwhile in Boston, relations between the Colonists and the King continued to deteriorate. On February 23, 1770, several Boston youths found a customs worker named Ebenezer Richardson on the street. They pelted him with stones and snowballs and then they broke all the windows in the house where he fled for refuge. Richardson fired a musket into the crowd of boys, killing one. A month later, a group of young men cornered a British sentry guarding a customs house on King Street and started throwing snowballs and chunks of ice at him. Other guards rushed to his defense. When the incident was over, five civilians were dead and six were wounded. This clash was called "The Boston Massacre" and it further escalated tensions between the British and the Colonists.

More political protest followed in 1773 when a group of Colonists disguised as Mohawk Natives boarded three British tea ships and dumped 342 chests of tea into Boston Harbor. They were protesting the fact that Britain had lowered the tax on tea giving British Tea a monopoly on the American Tea Trade. Colonists viewed this as an example of tyranny by the King. The King responded by closing Boston Harbor and the Colonists responded with additional acts of protest.

The Boston Tea Party on December 16, 1773. A group of Colonists disguised as Mohawk Warriors dumped 342 chests of English tea into Boston Harbor to protest the tyranny of the King.

Tensions escalated and in August 1775, when the Colonists around Massachusetts formed a Continental Army and gathered in a place called Dorchester Heights, which was at an elevation of 112 feet above the harbor and the town. While the British army waited for word from the King in London on how to proceed, a terrible winter began. The British discovered that if they did not replace the guards on duty every thirty minutes during a winter storm, the men would freeze to death while standing at their posts. Meanwhile, the Continental Army with George Washington as commander, made a daring plan.

During January and February, Continental soldiers pushed and dragged fifty-nine cannons from Ft. Ticonderoga in northern New York State 300 miles across ice and snow to Albany, then across the Berkshire Mountains to Dorchester Heights, 112 feet above the harbor and town of Boston. An imposing display of fire power was now in range of the city!

On March 5, the Continental Army made a surprise attack where the British were literally 'under the guns' of the Continentals and the British were forced to surrender. General Howe made a deal with Washington that if the British were allowed to sail out of Boston peacefully, the British would not set fire to the town. Washington agreed, and over the next two weeks, 120 ships were loaded with 8,900 soldiers and 1,100 fourth and fifth generation Loyalists who left Boston and sailed for Nova Scotia, joining Colonel Prince in the town of Digby. The people forced onto a ship at the last minute had to leave all their personal belongings behind. The Continental Loyalists and the British sailed away in total disgrace.

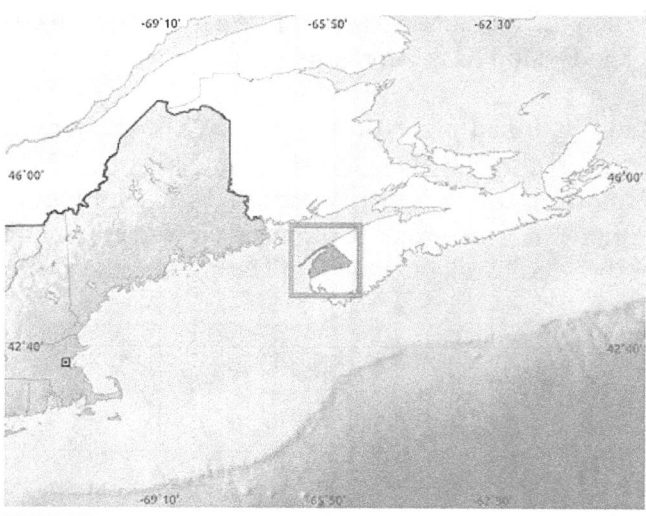

Digby, Nova Scotia is located due east of the state of Maine and 350 miles from Boston across open water.

John Prince, son of Christopher and Mary who had arrived in Nova Scotia as an infant, never returned to live in America when the Revolutionary War ended. He was raised in Nova Scotia as a British citizen and later married Sarah Willoughby. In 1784 they had a son who they named Christopher after his grandfather. Family records show that when Christopher was a very young man, his father John "disappeared in Canada and his mother died" leaving him to be raised by his Uncle Benjamin Prince who was a physician and a druggist. In about 1809, Uncle Benjamin Prince left Nova Scotia for New York City and took his young nephew Christopher with him. Christopher, like two of his great grandfathers before him, would "take to the sea" when he arrived in New York City. He became the family's last sea captain, Captain Christopher Prince.

In the 1700's Digby, Nova Scotia was a small fishing village. In 1783 many Loyalists left Boston and settled in the town, and it became a center for ship building.

Chapter 4
The Revolutionary War and the Battle of Brooklyn

An Ancient Map of Brooklyn details plots of farmland belonging to the original Dutch settlers in 1645. In the Northeast section, facing south, there is a drawing of a "Brooklyn Church."

This Ancient Map made before 1750 shows a Brooklyn Church in the upper right-hand corner. To the left of the Church by the East River are three houses and a high area of ground. This area was called Brooklyn Heights.

In 1749, Johannes De Bevoise and Hannah Betts married and moved to a farm "on the road to the ferry" next to the "Brooklyn Church" four miles north of the town of Flatbush. (5) Johannes was the grandson of Jacobus De Bevoise who first settled in Brooklyn as a child in 1659, the son of Carel De Bevoise, a County Judge in Brooklyn from 1752 – 1761. An oil painting of this farmhouse shows it standing to the right of the church. (Please refer to the front cover of this book for a full color illustration.) The painting also shows that the farmhouse was typical of Dutch houses built at this time. The house was built directly on the street with a fence running along the road. The house had a low ceiling and was a story and a half in height. The roof was heavy and was broken up by two dormer windows which allowed light inside. The roof extended over the front of the house to make a porch and extended low over the

The De Bevoise Farmhouse in 1749 was next to the Brooklyn Church, four miles north of Flatbush

back until it came within two or three feet of the ground. The rooms inside did not have a ceiling but had heavy beams on which the planks of the upper floor were laid. The entire house was heated by an open wood fireplace which was extremely large, and which extended the width of one wall so the entire family could have a seat in front of it. The chairs were made of dark, solid wood with broad seats covered in durable silk or brocade. The backs were high and straight with front legs terminating in claw feet clasping a ball. The chimney was exceptionally large so that meat could be hung inside to be smoked.

Another example of a Dutch homestead in Brooklyn at this time was Labon's Inn on Fulton Avenue built before the Revolutionary War, shown here in a drawing from 1833.

Large earthen glazed tiles imported from Holland were inset around the front of the fireplace. These tiles usually had scenes from the Bible painted on them. In the corner of the house there was always a spinning wheel so that flax and wool could be turned into yarn to make clothing. The early homes did not have carpets but had a light covering of beach sand over them so that they could be swept clean, then dried, spread over the floor, and swept clean again. In 1764, Johannes and Hannah gave birth to a daughter, Margaretta who was twelve when the Revolutionary War came to her front door.

Inside a Dutch farmhouse, the wood floors were bare. The large open wood fireplace was surrounded by earthenware glazed tiles from Holland; the family could sit here for warmth.

The British General Howe and the Colonial General George Washington both knew that seizing New York was the key to holding the entire American continent. General Howe made plans to gather his army in Nova Scotia and then sail south to attack New York. General Washington went immediately from Boston to New York to prepare for the British attack which he knew was imminent. As Washington and his generals surveyed the area around the city, they noticed that across the East River near the tiny town of Brooklyn there were seven or eight houses and an old Dutch Church that stood in the middle of the main road inland from the Brooklyn Ferry landing. From the New York side of the river, the village was out of site, but there was a "bluff" known as Brooklyn Heights, where one could stand on the Brooklyn side and look down on all of New York City, the harbor, the rivers, and the long low hills of New Jersey beyond. Washington believed that the key to the

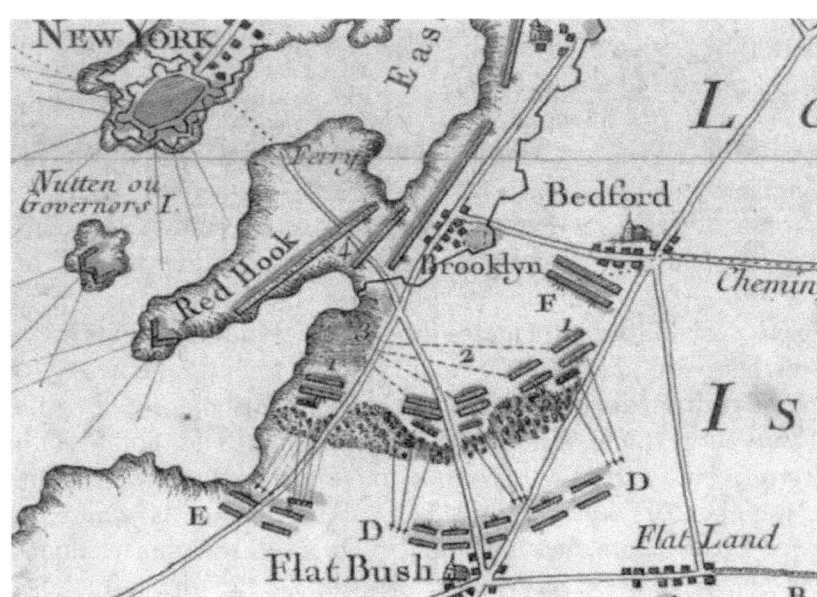

A military drawing of Brooklyn Heights showed the heavy fortifications built to the south of the tiny town to repel the British troops.

defense of Long Island was Brooklyn Heights, so he instructed his army to build fortifications along that section of the island. This location would prove to be extremely important to the general and his Army in the final days of the battle which was to come.

On July 2, 1776, the Continental Congress in Philadelphia voted to "dissolve the connection" the Continentals had with England and four days later this news reached New York City where spontaneous celebrations broke out among many of the people. Citizens and soldiers heard the words of the Declaration of Independence, and many were overjoyed that they were now fighting a war for an independent America in which "all men are created equal." They were particularly happy that there would no longer be a King to rule them. A large group of soldiers stormed down Broadway to Bowling Green where there was a gigantic statue of King George sitting on his colossal horse. They hacked off the King's head and placed it on a pike outside a tavern and melted the rest of the statue down to make bullets. Unfortunately, this carnival atmosphere, did not last long. In August 1776, General Howe arrived in New York Harbor with an armada of 400 ships, the largest force ever sent forth from England. People in the town exclaimed that the ships' masts were so numerous they looked like a forest of trees in winter. Washington was not certain whether Howe would first attack Manhattan or Long Island. He kept half of his army, including many of his best officers, in Manhattan.

In August 1776, an armada of 400 ships arrived in New York Harbor to attack the city of New York and end the American Revolution. The ships' masts were so numerous they looked like a forest of trees.

A 21-year-old Continental soldier from Franklin County Pennsylvania was sent to Brooklyn Heights with the 3rd Continental Artillery to build the heavy fortifications south of the tiny town. These fortifications would be needed if the British landed first on Long Island and began to attack. This young soldier was named Dr. John Duffield. John's father had emigrated to Pennsylvania from Ireland and John had come to New York to join the fight against the King as a surgeon and a member of Washington's staff. Family records claim that General Washington used the farmhouse of Johannes and Hannah De Bevoise as his headquarters during the Battle of Brooklyn, but this may not be accurate because the De Bevoise farmhouse was "on the road to the ferry" but was several miles to the east of Brooklyn Heights. However, during the building of fortifications, during the battle, or after the battle, John Duffield met twelve-year-old Margaretta De Bevoise because several years after the war, Margaretta and John were married.

If the British invaded Long Island, the Continental Army needed to do everything in its power to stop the advance. General Washington asked the farmers in Flatbush and nearby towns to drive their cattle to the eastern part of the Island and to take their grain, which had just been harvested, out of their barns and into the fields where it could be quickly and easily burned if necessary to avoid capture by the enemy. The farmers also dug a huge trench in front of the town and cut down an ancient white oak tree and dragged it across the main road. They hoped this would stop the British Army if it advanced toward the town. Everyone waited.

At daybreak, on August 22, four thousand of the King's elite troops landed on the southern tip of Long Island on the empty beach at Graveshead Bay. Pennsylvania riflemen posted near the shore quickly withdrew to warn the town of Flatbush, driving off cattle and burning wheat fields and farm buildings in their path as they ran. Wave after wave of red coated soldiers followed, their polished bayonets gleaming in the sunshine until 15,000 men and forty pieces of artillery had landed and were rapidly and smoothly assembled in perfect formation.

General Cornwallis pressed directly inland for six miles to establish a military camp in the little village of Flatbush, easily marching over the trench and the large fallen oak tree across the main road. As they marched into town, the British troops were amazed by what they saw: substantial farmhouses with fine furnishings, fields with mature peach and apple orchards, ample crops now set on fire; such affluence was a shock to them. They also noticed that the women and young children were not in town as they had all run to safety into Queens County and New Jersey. The British broke into the stone houses, made holes in the walls, and began firing their canons at the Colonial soldiers in the woods. The Battle of Brooklyn, the largest battle of the Revolutionary War, had begun.

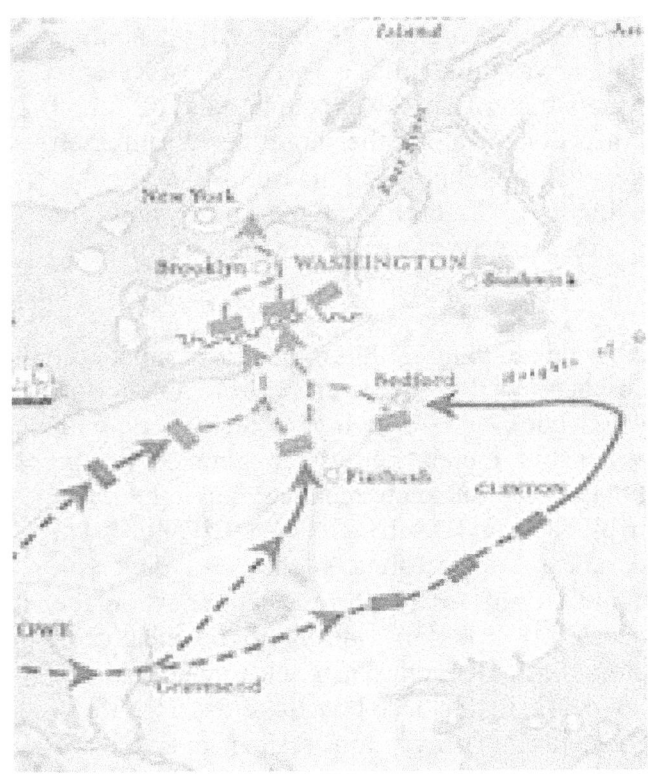

The British soldiers, shown in dark lines, attacked from the rear and the side, surrounding the Continental soldiers, pushing them north toward the East River. The Colonials lost 1,000 soldiers, the British lost only 400.

Washington had never commanded a large army and only two or three of his officers had ever faced an enemy in battle. Although his men fought well in the woods, they were not a well-trained fighting force and did not do well on the open ground. Washington had no cavalry to serve as his "eyes and ears," no spies, and no reliable intelligence to know where the enemy was making its advance. In the next three days of battle, General Howe skillfully maneuvered his army into a surprise attack from the rear and the side, throwing the Colonial soldiers into a panic. They fled north to Brooklyn Heights where they were trapped with their backs to the East River. On the evening of August 29, as the British prepared to storm the beach and decimate the remaining Colonial soldiers, a cold, drenching rain began to fall. The British army was forced to dig in and wait until dawn for the rain to stop. But the rain did not stop; in fact, it rained so hard, the Continental Army could not pitch tents, could not build fires to cook food, and the men had to fall asleep standing up. The next day the steady rain continued. Washington and his generals met at Brooklyn Heights overlooking the river and made a bold plan. They had lost over 1,000 men. They had no choice but to retreat and save what remained of the Army to fight another day. It was three miles across the East River to Manhattan. There were hundreds of small crafts docked along the shoreline. Washington decided to withdraw all his troops that night using these flat bottom boats, canoes, and rafts to cross the river to safety under cover of total darkness.

General George Washington prepared to withdraw his troops under cover of darkness across the East River to safety in Manhattan.

Miraculously, at 11:00pm the rain stopped, the winds died down and then shifted to the southeast. All available crafts were able to load horses, cannons, troops, and supplies and cross back and forth in the pitch dark with water but inches below the gunnels of the boats. One oarsman recalled making eleven trips back and forth across the river in total darkness and absolute silence. As daybreak came closer, several troops remained on the beach in Brooklyn waiting to be evacuated along with General Washington, who insisted on being in the last boat to cross to safety. Suddenly a heavy fog settled over all of Brooklyn concealing everything for exactly enough time for the final three boats to shove off toward Manhattan. In a single night 9,000 troops, horses and artillery had escaped across the river; not one life was lost. A Colonial sailor named Christopher Prince (no relation) onboard a nearby ship looked across the river as the sun rose and later described the incident as a miracle:

In a single night, 9,000 Colonial troops escaped across the East River to safety in Manhattan. The British made a huge mistake in this battle in that they never captured General George Washington.

"The Lord sending that heavy fog, and continued it so long, prevented nearly all from being made prisoners and many numbered among the dead. This interposition of Divine Providence, could not go unnoticed by the greatest infidel." (6)

As soon as the fog cleared, the British Red Coats swarmed down to the beach prepared to kill as many Continental soldiers as possible. They were amazed to see that the beach was empty; every soldier was gone.

The Revolutionary War would wage on for another seven years. Flatbush and Brooklyn would remain in the hands of the British and were subject to terrible destruction and theft. British authorities took property from the Colonists without ceremony: cattle, hogs, and chickens. Farmers told of horses being commandeered even as they were in the middle of ploughing a field! The church and the schoolhouse were turned into a prison and a hospital, as were some private homes. The people who lived in Flatbush could not openly aid the Revolutionary Cause, however they were able to help covertly by backing the newly formed government currency with their personal gold and silver. Records of these transactions had to be kept secret; one man received a signed note for a certain amount of money, and he put the note in a corked bottle and buried it under a fencepost outside his barn. A member of the Martense family advanced the largest amount of money during the war, an amount thought to have been close to $5500, a fortune at that time. The process of loaning money "to the Cause" continued until the Peace and bound everyone in the town close together because to tell anyone of these business dealings was to risk death. What is remarkable is that not a single person was ever betrayed or discovered.

After six years of war the British and Continental armies were exhausted. In Britain, the American conflict became unpopular and divisive. In the colonies, the long struggle led to enormous debt and food shortages. In 1781, General Nathaniel Greene fought the British in the Carolinas and forced them to march northeast. The British retreated to Yorktown, Virginia on the York River where they ran into a blockade from the French and American navies. General Washington then marched his troops to the north of the town and the British were surrounded and forced to surrender. This victory for the Continental Army finally led to negotiations for peace with the signing of the Treaty of Paris in 1783.

George Washington (on left) received the sword of Lord Cornwallis in surrender at the Battle of Yorktown which was a victory for the Colonial Army and the birth of the United States of America.

Chapter 5

Captain Christopher Prince - Maritime Adventurer

In 1787, four years after the Revolutionary War ended, Dr. John Duffield left the Continental Army and married Margaretta De Bevoise whom he had met at her family's farm near Brooklyn Heights. (7) They moved to a farm half a mile north of the De Bevoise homestead and had three daughters: Anna, Susan, and Margaretta. We have four family antiques that were present in the Duffield house at this time: before her marriage, Margaretta owned a very decorative Banjo Clock with a circular hand painted tin dial and Roman chapters. There was also a Chippendale mahogany side chair with claw and ball feet and the Roman numeral VIII carved on the inside. This was most likely part of a set of eight dining chairs and a large dining table. (8) There were also two elaborate mirrors: a large gilt mahogany wall mirror with an eagle pediment (pictured on this page) and a huge George II style gilt pier glass mirror with a phoenix bird over the top. People imagine a Dutch farmhouse as containing only the bare necessities of life, but this was not true.

American mahogany Banjo Clock, circa 1780 belonged to Margaretta De Bevoise, a very rare and fragile antique.

Dr. John Duffield had a fine homestead, and he also had three daughters who needed husbands. At that time, it was a short trip to Brooklyn Heights where the family would then take the ferry across the East River to the docks at Water Street in New York City. The family made this trip from time to time because all three of the daughters eventually married ships' captains: Susan married Captain Charles Lawrence, Margaretta married Captain Archibald Thompson and after his death Samuel Willoughby, and Anna married Captain Christopher Prince, who had recently arrived from Nova Scotia. The girls settled close to their parents. The Brooklyn streets that run through what was formerly Duffield property to this day have family names: Duffield, Lawrence, Willoughby, Prince.

A miniature portrait in a gold locket frame painted on ivory of a young Captain Christopher Prince still exists. (Please refer to the front cover of this book for a color illustration.) It shows a fine-featured, debonair young man with light brown hair. It was intended, at the time, as a talisman suitable to be worn by a fiancée or wife. (Concealed behind the gold casing is a commemorative lock of the subject's hair.)

Gilt mahogany wall mirror with prominent eagle pediment

Captain Prince commanded ships owned or managed by N.L. & G. Griswold, 72 South Street, New York. According to his *Ship's Log*, Christopher's first recorded voyage was in 1806 when he was twenty-two. He sailed from Capetown to New York on the ship **Rebecca**, then several months later he sailed **Rebecca** from New York to Boston and then to Marseilles. The only cargo he mentioned in his *Ship's Log* was pepper and cotton. His voyages continued from Cuba to Sumatra and St. Petersburg to Buenos Aires. In 1811 Captain Christopher married Anna Duffield and over the next twelve years of marriage they had six children, three girls: Margaret Amelia Prince, Anna De Bevoise Prince, and Susan Lawrence Prince (9), and three boys: Benjamin, Christopher, and John Duffield De Bevoise Prince. (10)

Captain Christopher Prince from Nova Scotia, moved to New York City and became a sea captain in early 1800.

Captain Christopher Prince continued to sail from New York to Cuba and Buenos Aires. At one point in his voyages, he saved the lives of a shipwrecked crew and was presented with a silver tankard as a token of appreciation. Family records tell that Captain Prince died young, but we do not know exactly where or when this happened. His *Ship's Log* states that sometime in 18—he died "On home voyage four days out of Port." The name of the ship, the port, and the date were not recorded.

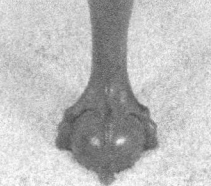

Chippendale San Dominican mahogany side chair, 1760 with claw and ball front feet from the home of Dr. John Duffield, later known in the family as "The Washington Chair"

Chapter 6
The Reign of Cruelty and the End of Slavery in New York

At the beginning of the Nineteenth Century, two major advances came to New York which had a positive effect on the Five Dutch Towns of Kings County. The first development happened on July 4, 1827, when the institution of Slavery was abolished in New York State.

Freedom for all African Americans was long overdue. The first Blacks who landed on Manhattan Island in 1625 were eleven African captives of the Dutch West Indian Company. Slaves built the original road between lower Manhattan and Harlem and worked the fields and estates of what was then underdeveloped marshland and countryside. As more Africans were shipped in to build the Colony, the majority were concentrated in lower Manhattan where they continued to clear timber and construct the city's roads and buildings.

The Dutch brought the first 11 slaves to Manhattan in 1625. Slaves built the city's first roads and buildings.

Residents of the small town of Flatbush relied on the labor of enslaved people to clear forests and to build houses, churches, towns, and roads. The price of a slave at that time in New York was between $100 and $150. Some residents were wealthy enough to own their own slaves; others "rented" company slaves provided by the Dutch West Indian Company. In the 1698 census, the Lefferts family reported three enslaved people in their household. The Vanderbilt and Martense families also owned large farms in the area, so they must have owned or rented slaves and benefitted from their labor for generations.

As the agricultural economy expanded, so did the number of slaves. In the years before the Revolutionary War, the population of Flatbush grew to 551 white people, 378 enslaved people, and twelve free Black people. Gertrude Lefferts Vanderbilt, related by birth and by marriage to two of the largest land-owning families in the area, defended the use of slaves as a necessity. In her book, *The Social History of Flatbush*

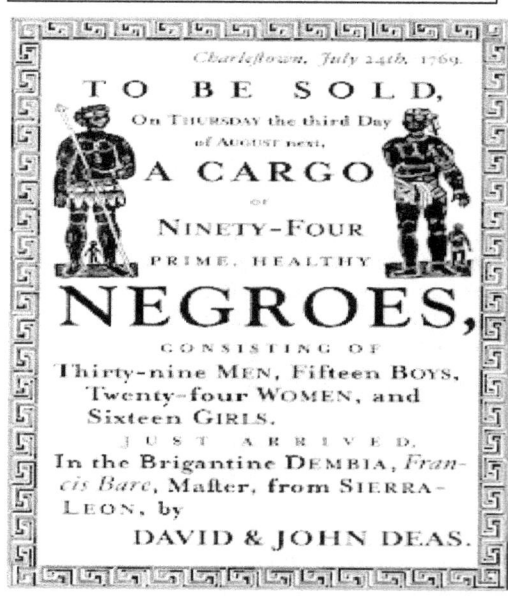

An advertisement for a slave auction in 1769 in Charleston, SC

written in 1899, she wrote that "there were a number of colored people in every family, they were slaves, but it was a light form of slavery:" (11) She continues to claim that:

"The institution of Slavery was one that commended itself to the Dutch mind rather as a necessity than as a desirable system; a milder form of it among the Dutch of New Netherlands can scarcely be imagined. If a slave was dissatisfied with his master, it was very common for the master to give him a paper on which his age and his price were written and allow him to go and look for someone with whom he would prefer to live, and who would be willing to pay the price stated. When the slave found a purchaser, the master completed the arrangement by selling his discontented slave to the person whom he preferred." (12)

This drawing showed the cruelty of a slave auction. Children were usually separated from their parents and sold to different owners. Slave families were divided and never saw one another again.

Dr. Thomas Strong, Pastor of the Reformed Dutch Church of Flatbush in 1842, did not share Mrs. Lefferts Vanderbilt's benign view of human bondage. He referred to Slavery as "the Reign of Cruelty and Terror" (13) and in his book, *The History of Flatbush*, he thanked God that it had passed away.

In 1781, a law was passed in New York that freedom would be given to any able-bodied Negro man who had fought in certain regiments during the Revolutionary War for three years or until regularly discharged. Finally in 1817, the New York legislature declared that all enslaved people in New York State would be freed in ten years, on July 4, 1827. Emancipation in 1827 set free 10,000 slaves in Manhattan and Long Island. In Flatbush, many who were former slaves found employment as domestics or as laborers on the farms where they previously had been enslaved. These former slaves would not be given the right to vote until 1870, five years after the end of the Civil War.

The second most important advance was the opening of the Erie Canal in 1825. "The Atlantic's Back Door is Open" said one newspaper. The gigantic canal allowed for speedy and very inexpensive transport of grain from farmlands in the Midwest directly to the port of New York City. In Flatbush, the farmers no longer needed to grow grain, so they could concentrate on produce: cabbage, potatoes, fruits, and vegetables. These crops were sent directly across the East River into the growing city of New York.

Before 1825, landowners retained their farms and did not divide their property into individual "city lots;" however, the land around Brooklyn and Flatbush gradually became more valuable. The town of Flatbush built a new Dutch Reformed Church where services were given in English, a Court House, and a college named Erasmus Hall certified by the State of New York which taught both young men and young women. People in the town began to build sidewalks along the main road and many houses that had been standing before the Revolutionary War were torn down to make way for many more beautiful and spacious dwellings.

Chapter 7

John Duffield Prince and Helen Martense - A Brilliant Marriage and a Successful Business

On January 13, 1835, John Duffield Prince, son of Captain Christopher Prince and Anna Duffield, married Gertrude Helen Martense, a young woman from one of the most prolific families in Flatbush. Gertrude's mother was Helen Van Brunt, a descendant of Rutgert Joosten Van Brunt, who settled in New Utrecht in 1657. Mrs. Helen Van Brunt Martense was known in the community as "public spirited and generous, taking an active part in whatever tended to the public good and to the cause of benevolence." (14) Gertrude's father was George Martense whose family was the original "son of Martin" and one of the largest landowners in the area. Their wedding would have adhered to all the Dutch customs at the time. First, the bride would receive a tea service consisting of a teapot, cream pitcher, sugar bowl, and fruit compote. These were usually of heavy, solid silver and varied in price according to the means of the family. Fortunately, the tea service which belonged to Gertrude Helen Martense is still in our family and her maiden-name initials < G M > are clearly visible. The reason for the use of the maiden-name initials was

Gertrude Martense Prince in the simple dark dress in fashion for married women in the Dutch town of Flatbush in 1845.

that traditionally Dutch women held significant property rights. Wives were considered co-owners of family property, and daughters were entitled to half of their parents' estate. Under English Common Law, sons received inheritance priority and widows were entitled to only one-third of their husband's real property. Even after English rule, many Dutch families in New York maintained a more egalitarian outlook for women. In our family, we followed Dutch custom and always referred to this ancestor by her maiden name: "Gertrude Martense" even though she was married to a Prince for over fifty years.

Weddings in Dutch families were celebrated in the house of the bride's parents. The service was performed in the early evening with only immediate relatives of the bride and groom; the invited guests came soon after. There was always a huge feast with younger guests staying at the house until after midnight. It was the

The Martense Tea Set, antique American silver, Marquand & Co., New York 1830

custom for the bride and groom to wear their wedding clothes to Church the next day and usually they would try to wear clothes that were the same color, dark or light blue was extremely popular. The bride could receive an engagement ring, but it was optional; she could also receive a wedding ring, usually a gold band although it was not used in the Church ceremony. In the Dutch community, peace and harmony in the household were taken for granted.

"Peace and harmony were the normal condition of things. The reverse would have been commented upon as something of unusual occurrence." (15)

When John and Gertrude married, he was twenty-one and she was sixteen. They lived for about a year with Gertrude's parents in the Martense Homestead on the New Utrecht Road, near Church Lane. During this time, John founded the firm of ***John D. Prince and Sons***, dealers in paints and oils, on lower Fulton Street, Brooklyn, the principal business section of the city.

The next year, on the corner of Fulton Avenue and Clarkson Street, an old tavern was torn down, and John and Gertrude began construction of a beautiful, spacious house. Gertrude Lefferts Vanderbilt writing at the time remarked that the grounds of the house were "exceedingly ornamental to the village. The separating fences between the neighbors have been removed and the gardens thrown into one, an act of significant friendly feeling." (16) Mary Martense Prince wrote a short family history in 1905 where she described the house as "The house we all remember, with wings on either side and the pleasant piazzas." She then described in detail the gardens of the house:

An early photograph of the Prince home, circa 1837 on the corner of Fulton Avenue and Clarkson Street. Large magnolia trees stood on either side of the stone steps. The house stood for about 100 years before being torn down to make room for a group of shops.

"In the spring the large oval flower bed in front of the house was a mass of bloom with brilliant tulips and hyacinths, and over these flowers would be falling like large snowflakes the leaves of the magnolia trees that stood on either side of the stone steps. As we entered the gate, we pass under one of the pretty little arbors that later were covered with the deep pink globes of the prairie rose. At the south side of the house, we would stop to pick some of the fragrant double violets, or tiny Johnny-jump-ups, and to see if the lilies of the valley were in bloom."

The life of the John Duffield Prince family in this home was the epitome of understated style and comfort. A large oil painting of Gertrude was commissioned and placed in the home. (Please refer to the front cover of this book for a color illustration.) Gertrude's dark colored dress in the painting showed the fashion for married women at that time which was very simple and practical. The bonnet on her head had two rows of white lace trim, no other lace, bows, or jewelry were visible.

The house was "hospitable, with several guest rooms where relatives and friends were often entertained; where everyone is friendly, that is filled with young people and neighbors who always seem like members of the family," wrote Mary Martense Prince. When Gertrude's father died, her mother Helen and her unmarried younger sister Esther left the Martense Homestead and "removed to the residence of her son-in-law Mr. John Duffield Prince where she lived until her death." (17) The Martense Homestead was then given to her brother, Jacob Van Brunt Martense. In this manner, homes often stayed in the families of the original Dutch settlers for generations.

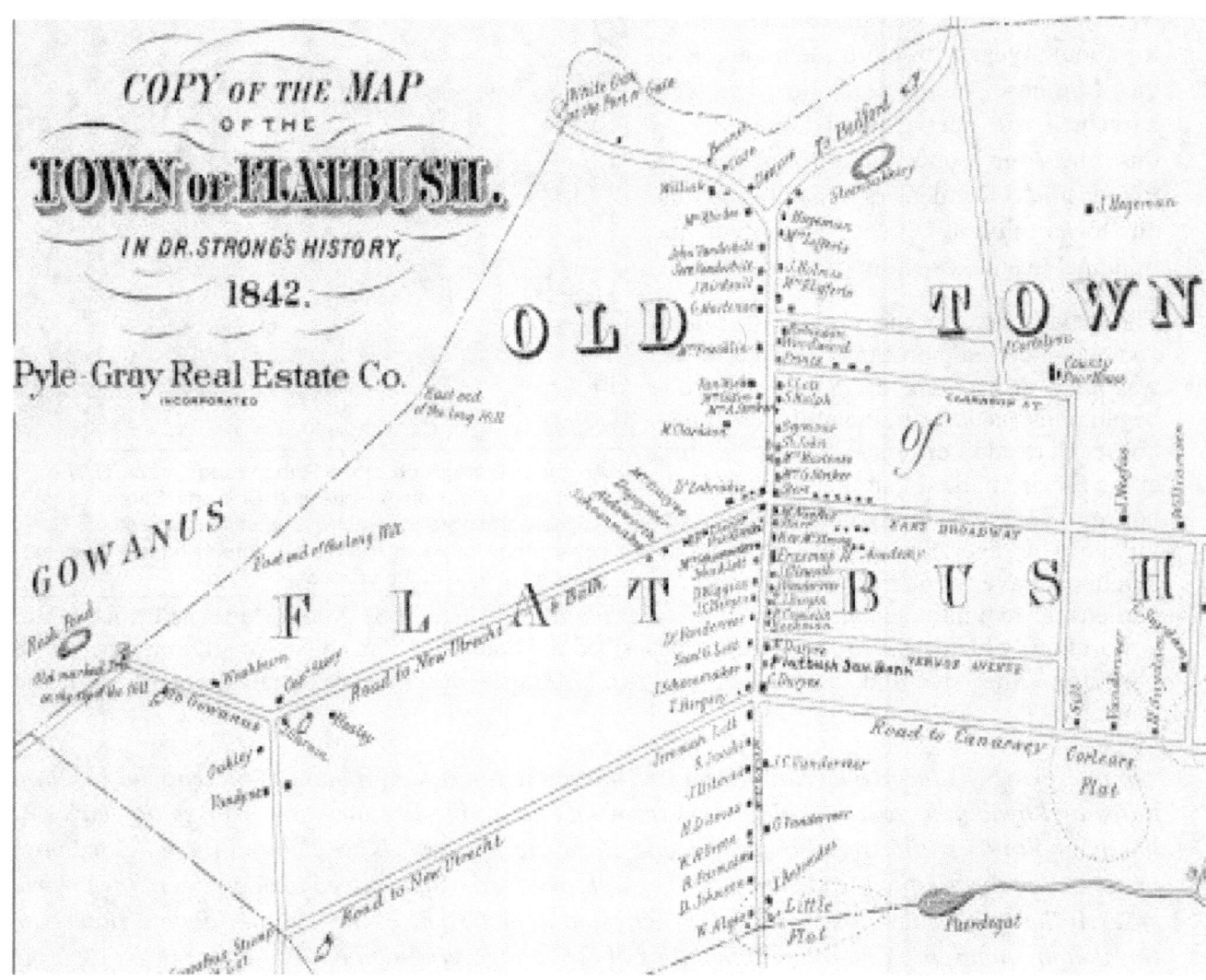

The Town of Flatbush in 1842; the Prince home was on the corner of Fulton and Clarkson. Two hundred years after the town was first settled, families along Fulton Street continued to have the names of the original Dutch settlers: Martense, Lefferts, Hegeman, Ditmas, Vanderveer and Vanderbilt.

Two years after John and Gertrude's marriage, George Prince was born followed closely by Christopher and Adrian. A fourth son, Jacob Van Brunt Prince was born in 1844 followed by two children who died in infancy: Benjamin and Helen. Esther, Gertrude, John, and another Helen were all born during the next 10 years. For over 25 years John Duffield Prince served as the Superintendent of the Sunday School as well as Deacon, Elder and Choirmaster while Gertrude was Superintendent of the Infant Department. This achievement was remarkable because the Dutch Reformed Church was the most important social and spiritual institution in the town. In his spare time, John would carve tiny plum pits so skillfully and intricately that he was able to gift them to relatives and friends to wear as earrings and pins.

John and Gertrude were married for fifty two years, and the firm ***John D. Prince and Sons*** flourished for three generations with the boys in the family working at the store. As Prince sea captains in the past, all the boys "took to the sea" and were skilled sailors. They had a succession of boats named ***Princess*** and they often took their boats out to the Upper Bay, the Lower Bay, and as far as Rockaway Beach to bring home "sheepshead" fish and oysters for dinner.

New York City grew dramatically during this time. Architect Frederick Olmsted began building the 843-acre Central Park where city inhabitants could walk and enjoy the natural looking plants and landforms. Across the East River, the Five Dutch Towns of Kings County were still rather rustic and contained a great sweep of open countryside that had not changed much from 1750 – 1850.

This Plum Pit was hand carved by John Duffield Prince. It was one inch high and ½ an inch wide.

Looking at the Map of the Town of Flatbush in 1842, many of the families along Fulton Street had the names of the original three families from the late 1600's: Lefferts, Vanderbilt, and Martense, as well as other Dutch settlers who came to town soon after: Vanderveer, Schoonmaker, Ditmas, Neefus, Striker, and Hegeman.

Antique silver cup (left) reads: *"Jacob Van Brunt Prince from his uncle Jacob Van Brunt Martense, 1844"* illustrates how names were often passed down from one generation to the next. A portrait of the benefactor uncle (JVB Martense) appears on the right.

Chapter 8

Ellen Babcock Prince - A Woman of Independent Means and Her Generous Brother William

In 1850 the town of Flatbush remained sheltered and isolated. Separated by the East River from the frenzy of Manhattan, it was gaining an urban gloss just as the rest of America was entering its most difficult and divisive period.

Whereas slavery had been abolished in the Northern States, it remained law in the Southern States making America "a house divided." In 1850, Congress passed the **Fugitive Slave Act** which prohibited the citizens in the Northern "free" States from giving shelter or assistance to any slaves who escaped from plantations in the South.

As a young girl, Harriet Beecher Stowe, daughter of an outspoken Calvinist preacher and our ancestor on the Danforth side of the family, (18) was privileged to receive a traditional academic education at the Hartford Seminary. At this time, such a thorough education was given to boys only. In 1832 Harriet moved with her family to Cincinnati Ohio, the western town that was on its way to becoming the sixth largest city in America.

Trade and shipping were booming, drawing migrants from various parts of the country, including "escaped slaves." Harriet met African Americans in Cincinnati who were fearful that they would be captured by bounty hunters and sent back to the South. She wrote: *"The time has come where even a woman or a child who can speak a word for freedom and humanity, is bound to speak."*

In 1851, at age 40 and mother to seven children, Harriet wrote the American Classic, *Uncle Tom's Cabin*. The book painted a word picture of Slavery, causing readers in the Northern States to have a great deal of empathy for the slaves in the story and by extension for all enslaved peoples. It became an anti-slavery bombshell and was a runaway success, selling 10,000 copies in its first week and over 300,000 copies by the end of the year. The only book to outsell it at the time was the *Bible*.

Harriet Beecher Stowe was our ancestor and author of *Uncle Tom's Cabin*. This anti-slavery drama was a landmark in protest literature and was one of the elements which started the Civil War.

From 1851 – 1861 tensions between North and South continued to rise. The crisis came to a head when South Carolina seceded from the Union in 1861 at the Battle of Fort Sumter. A year later when President Abraham Lincoln met Harriet Beecher Stowe, he was reported as saying to her, *"So you are the little woman who wrote the book that started this great war."*

John Duffield Prince and Gertrude Martense Prince's two oldest boys, George and Christopher would have been old enough to fight for the North in the Civil War. To my knowledge, neither man became a Union soldier, but another ancestor was a significant help to the Northern Alliance of States. In 1861, during the peak of the Industrial Revolution, 18-year-old William Augustus Babcock from South Coventry, Connecticut began an apprenticeship to become a machinist. In 1862 he tried to enlist in the Union Army, but he was told that with his skill as a machinist, he would be more useful making firearms for the Northern Alliance of States. Thus, William remained a civilian in Connecticut, working in the Norwich Arms Company for the duration of the war. (19) When it ended, four years later, he became a traveling salesman selling machinery, railway supplies and machinist tools into markets that were booming from then astonishing advances in metallurgy and technology.

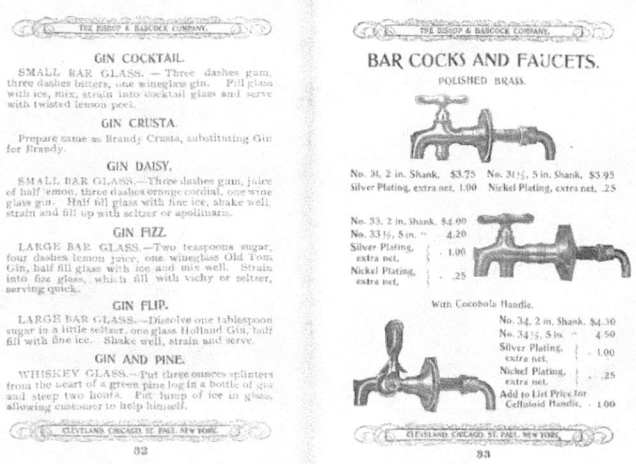

Catalogue from the Bishop and Babcock Company which made air compressors, beer pumps, bicycle pumps and fire extinguishers.

William became known as a "capable and sagacious businessman." In 1876, eleven years after the end of the Civil War, he married Gertrude Bunker from Brooklyn, New York. A year later they moved to the then flourishing industrial stronghold of Cleveland, Ohio. During the next four years William founded *The Standard Tool Company, The Cleveland Tack Works,* and, with Mr. K.D. Bishop, a businessman from Connecticut, the ***Bishop and Babcock Company*** which manufactured air compressors, beer pumps and faucets, bicycle pumps and hand fire extinguishers. The business was located on the corner of Kirtland and Hamilton Streets in Cleveland and had offices in New York, Chicago, and St. Paul, Minnesota.

William Babcock had two sisters: Mary Elizabeth and Ellen Harriet who continued to live quietly on the family's farm in South Coventry, Connecticut. As William was making a fortune in Cleveland, it became apparent that he and his wife would never have children. Possibly because of this fact, William became known as "a liberal benefactor wanting only to add to the comfort of others." During this time, he gave a generous sum of money to each of his two sisters enabling them to have an inheritance of their own and making them both women of "independent means."

In about 1871, at the age of twenty-five, Ellen married Irving Spaulding, a Connecticut farmer who was ten years her senior. The next year Irving died, and Ellen, now a young widow with no children, began the task of finding another husband. Her brother William's wife, Gertrude Bunker Babcock, was originally from Brooklyn, New York, and she may have been the one to orchestrate the introduction of Ellen to Jacob Van Brunt Prince of Flatbush who had lost his young wife Elizabeth Vanderbilt Spader several years earlier when he was twenty-six.

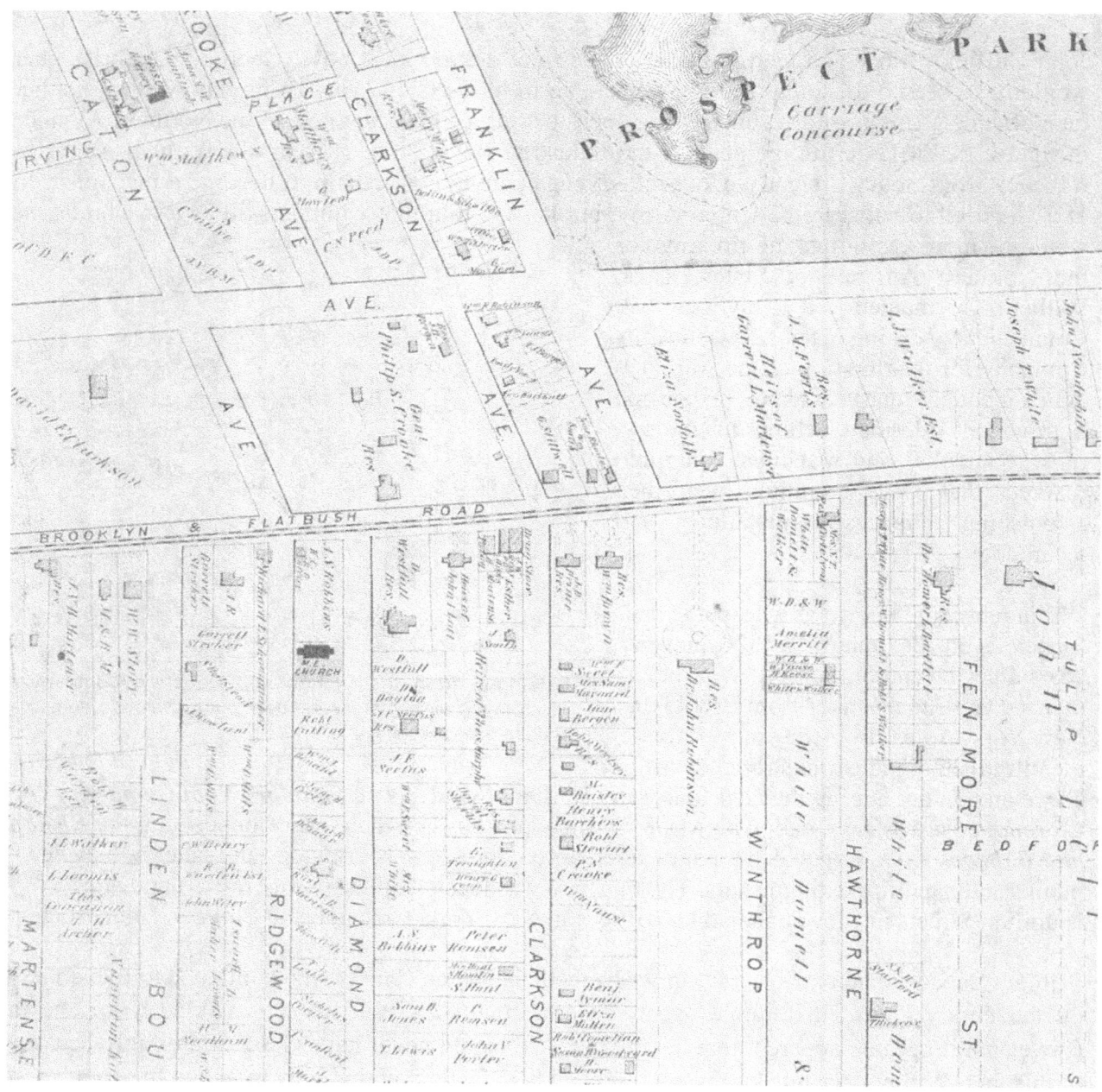

The Town of Flatbush in 1873, eight years after the end of the Civil War, had a large population. The streets were much more defined, and the land was divided into "city lots." The John Duffield Prince house was in the center of this map on the corner of Clarkson and the Brooklyn & Flatbush Road. Notice Martense Street four blocks to the south of Clarkson next to the home of Jacob Van Brunt Martense.

Jacob was a good match for Ellen. He was the son of John Duffield and Gertrude Martense Prince, he had been educated in "the Brooklyn schools," and as a young man he worked for his father at ***John D. Prince and Sons*** selling paints, oils, and varnish. He was a widower and he and his first wife had had no children.

Ellen was in the enviable position of having "independent financial means." Among other assets, her family owned a large dairy farm in South Coventry, Connecticut. John and Gertrude Prince would have approved of their son marrying such a well-established wife who was known to be incredibly fun loving and devoted to her family. She would also prove to be very independent and exceptionally outspoken. My father relayed a family story about a time when Ellen was introduced to a socially conscious young couple about to be married. Ellen regarded the young woman skeptically and then said to everyone present that "it was a good thing that (the young couple) were soon to be married because the soon-to-be-bride was obviously pregnant." At the time, everyone was shocked by this comment, but five months later, the young wife gave birth to a healthy child!

In 1876, 32-year-old Jacob Van Brunt Prince and the prosperous Ellen Harriet Babcock were married. Three years later their only child, a son, was born. Ellen broke with tradition in that she did not choose a name for her son from her husband's side of the family. Instead she named her son William Babcock Prince after her benefactor and very generous brother, William Babcock.

This DAR Pin (Daughters of the American Revolution) belonged to Ellen Babcock whose grandfather Ephraim fought in the Revolutionary War with the State of Connecticut when he was 15 years old.

Young "Will" was the center of his mother's life. Once when Will was a child he became sick and had to stay home from school for a week. To keep Will amused, Ellen took him to the movies every afternoon until he was better. The fact that Will may have been contagious to others did not concern her.

On May 24, 1883, the majestic Brooklyn Bridge, with its impressive Gothic towers, was finished at enormous expense of wealth and human labor. Prior to its construction, the only means of transit between the booming boroughs of Manhattan and Brooklyn was by boat. Now traveling across the span of the mighty bridge, a pedestrian could cover that distance in a few minutes. Brooklyn was no longer sheltered and isolated from Manhattan.

In time, Will's father Jacob became a prosperous manufacturer of fabricated industrial parts and fittings. The small family moved to a beautiful brownstone at the then fashionable 115 Montague Street in Brooklyn Heights. In the summer, mother and son would escape the heat of the city and visit the family farm in Connecticut.

The Brooklyn Bridge with its beautiful Gothic towers is a National Historic Landmark. Built in 1883, it finally allowed people to walk from Brooklyn to Manhattan in a few minutes.

A rare photograph of a handsome, young Will (facing the camera) shows him on the porch at their farm. Following his father's interest in engineering and metallurgy, Will attended Brooklyn Polytechnic for high school and then went to college at Stevens Institute of Technology in Hoboken, New Jersey graduating in 1900 with a degree in mechanical engineering and a varsity letter in lacrosse. Upon graduation he moved to Cleveland where he joined his uncle's company, **Bishop and Babcock**, soon becoming a director.

William Augustus Babcock, "The Elder" unfortunately, never lived to mentor his young nephew and namesake. While on a hunting trip to Wyoming in 1895 with a group of friends, the guide asked Mr. Babcock to dismount from his horse and walk the narrow trail ahead with mountains on one side and a steep precipice on the other because the trail had become wet and slippery. With a touch of arrogance, Mr. Babcock ignored this advice. He allegedly made the comment, "I paid for this horse, and I am going to ride him!" Almost immediately his horse fell to its knees. As the horse and rider tried to regain their footing, both fell over the steep cliff. All members of the hunting party rushed down the steep side of the cliff and found to their horror that the horse had fallen on top of its rider and survived the fall, but Mr. Babcock had serious internal injuries and did not have long to live. His last words were, "Boys, I am going, it is over with me. I am to blame. I thought I was a horseman, but I am not."

William Babcock Prince *(left)* and his father **Jacob Van Brunt Prince** *(far right)* at their farm in South Coventry, Connecticut. The gentleman in the middle may be Will's uncle, William Augustus Babcock.

This picture shows **a narrow trail in the Grand Canyon** in the 1890's with mountains on one side and a steep precipice on the other side.

Chapter 9

William Babcock Prince - Industrialist and Man About Town

After graduating from college in 1900, Will relocated to Cleveland, Ohio, quickly becoming a director in his late uncle's manufacturing firm, **Bishop and Babcock**. (My dad once remarked to me, *"Can you imagine a young man just out of college walking into his first job as a director? It probably shook the place up a bit!"*)

Will soon became known as an active leader in the community and one of its most eligible bachelors. A newspaper at the time referred to him as "the well-known clubman of Cleveland." He was a member of the Country Club, the Union Club, and the University Club. (20) He was a voracious reader, finishing a book almost every week. He avidly followed the Brooklyn "Trolley" Dodgers baseball team, and he loved to fish. The passion which consumed him for the rest of his life, however, was the machine later known as the automobile.

Catalogue from Bishop and Babcock Co, 1902

In 1908, the Model T was introduced to the world by the Ford Motor Company. It was simple to operate, affordable at the cost of $500, and surprisingly durable. The car started by turning a hand crank in front and it had no gas gauge, so the owner had to guess when it needed a fill up. Will bought the first Model T he could get his hands on, and he continued to purchase new model "machines" as they became available. A horse and buggy could travel at a speed of about eight miles per hour; the Model T would travel at a top speed of 40 – 45 miles per hour. A favorite family anecdote relays how Will, while driving the car with his wife as passenger, was reprimanded by her saying, *"Slow down, Will, you're driving over forty!"*

In the summer of 1912, Will boarded a train in Cleveland to visit a ranch he owned in Manitou, Colorado. On the train, he met a group of five schoolgirls from St. Louis who were also traveling West for a stay in Manitou under the watchful eyes of two chaperones: Miss Gertrude Crocker and Miss Helen Christie. Miss Gertrude Crocker had been a schoolteacher for many years; Miss Helen Christie, had been a schoolteacher at Wyman School for three years.

Helen's father, Edward Harris Christie was originally from Helena, Arkansas. At the end of the Civil War Edward's father, Edward Giles Christie, told his son that he should go

Miss Gertrude Crocker and **Miss Helen Christie** were chaperones for a group of five schoolgirls traveling West by train from St. Louis to Colorado during summer vacation.

to college in the North so that he could "learn to get along with Yankees." Edward was accepted at Pennsylvania State College (later Penn State University) and graduated in 1878 with a BA and MA in the Arts. He remained at the school for several years after graduation as an assistant professor of classical languages. It was there he met his future wife, Mary Margaret Mitchell. (21) The couple was married in 1884 and moved to St. Louis where Edward became principal of the Hodgen School, a public school in the downtown area. Eventually the family moved to a modest two-story house on 5069 Kensington Avenue. In his spare time Edward was a dedicated "student of birds" spending much of his free time roaming the countryside to locate and watch birds.

Born in 1885, Helen Christie was the oldest of three children and had graduated from Central High School before becoming a teacher. Helen was an extremely attractive young lady. She was tall and very slender with thick red hair and a classically beautiful face. Helen had been courted by several young men in town but was in no hurry to marry. She once told me: *"Never marry the first man who asks you."* As a young girl, she wore her beautiful red hair in a braid down her back. One day, the boy sitting behind her in school took a pair of scissors and cut the thick curly lock from the end of her braid. Helen was shocked and embarrassed, then surprised ten years later when the young man proposed marriage and handed her an envelope where he had kept her curly lock safe.

Mary Margaret Mitchell was granddaughter to "The Lady Who was Captured by Warriors."

Another story she told was of a young beau who came to her house in 1898, picked her up off her feet and swung her around in a circle saying, "Helen, I'm going to War!" The war that had captured this young man's imagination was the Spanish-American War in Cuba with the charismatic Teddy Roosevelt and his all-volunteer cavalry called the Rough Riders. Tragically, 385 young Americans died in battle during the four-month conflict in Cuba, but even more heartbreaking were the 2615 young men who died of typhoid and yellow fever, and that is what happened to Helen's beau. *"He never made it into battle,"* she told me. *"He died of fever the minute he landed in Cuba."*

The trip West on the train took several days, just enough time for the charming Will to become acquainted with the lovely Helen. A long-distance romance began and the following year, on April 26, 1913, they were married in St Louis in the presence of 150 guests at the bride's home. An article in the St Louis paper had the headline: *"Helen Christie, School Teacher, Meets Rich Ranch Owner and Wedding Bells Ring."* The article goes on to mention that the marriage to Mr. Prince would "doubtless open the arms of exclusive circles for his young bride." The bride's

Helen Christie Prince was 28 years old when she married Will Prince at her parents' home in St. Louis in 1913.

dress was described as "the conventional white *charmeuse*, veiled in part with an old Venetian lace and silver brooch." After their six-week honeymoon trip East, they went to live in Cleveland. A sad note to the end of that year was the death of Will's father, Jacob Van Brunt Prince in Brooklyn on November 8, 1913. A newspaper article said that Jacob spent the summer at the family home in South Coventry, Connecticut, and when he returned to Brooklyn, he took ill and died of a heart ailment. After the loss of her husband, Ellen moved to Connecticut full time. She remained fun loving and independent well into her later years, a favorite friend to her grandchildren. She also became interested in collecting fine art and elegant furnishings. (22) When she reached the age of 90, she moved to Cleveland to spend her last remaining years living with her two grandchildren, her beloved only child, Will and her daughter-in-law, Helen Christie Prince.

Will and Helen first lived in a modest home on 11409 Bellflower Road between the Cleveland Museum of Art and Lakeview Cemetery. Will founded the **Prince & Izant Company**, a metal products agency and Helen settled down to days filled with the social obligations expected of her. Helen was twenty-eight, Will was thirty-four, and they were anxious to start a family. In 1914, Helen gave birth to a son who died within a few days of his birth. He was given the name "Sonny" and he was buried in the Babcock / Prince family plot in Nathan Hale Cemetery in Coventry, Connecticut. Then in December 1917, a second son was born. He was named Edward Mitchell Prince, Edward for Helen's father and Mitchell for Helen's mother's family, Mary Margaret Mitchell who had died when Helen was seventeen. From the moment of his birth, everyone called the newborn by his nickname, "Ned."

Will and **Ned Prince, 1922**. Ned wore the "sailor suit" made popular in the 1920's by the British, Russian, and Swedish royal families.

Chapter 10

Edward Mitchell Prince - The Well-Mannered Only Son of an Only Son

Like his father before him, young Edward Mitchell Prince "Ned" was the center of his mother's life. In 1920 the family built an eight-bedroom, four bath, 4,000 square foot home at 2215 Harcourt Drive near Case Western Reserve University in Cleveland. Prohibition was the law of the land from 1920 – 1933. My father's earliest memory of this house was of men in a "flashy car" pulling into the back of the property and unloading cases of "illegal" liquor. He remembered one the men patted him on the head and said, "Hi there, Sonny" before driving away. Harcourt Drive was lined with stately homes full of large families, except for the Prince family.

2215 Harcourt Drive was a classically beautiful home near Case Western Reserve University

Will had been raised in Flatbush as an only child but he had had countless cousins, aunts, and uncles who lived nearby. There was no extended family living in Cleveland for young Ned.

In 1924 when Ned was seven, Will asked Dr. Chauncey Wycoff, Ned's pediatrician, if he knew of a suitable child who might be available for adoption. Helen had suffered several traumatic miscarriages after Ned's birth. Dr. Wycoff knew of an adorable two-year-old child, who was available. Will and Helen visited the child and felt an instant connection with her; they took her home and adopted her. My dad remembered stopping at the store to buy bottles, diapers, and baby clothes. They named her Ellen Babcock Prince after Will's mother.

In the 1920's during Prohibition, **Bishop and Babcock** was forced to change its business model from alcoholic drinks to more practical products like Auto Engine Cleaner.

"Ellie" grew extremely close to her mother and father during her childhood and into her adult life. She recalled to her children that her father Will used to call her "my little French girl" because he and Helen had been told by the adoption agency that her biological father was a French chef. After Helen died, my Aunt Ellie told me that she had found her adoption papers and that she could trace and find her birth family, but she had no interest in doing so. Years later, her daughter Avis did some research and discovered that Ellie's birth father's name was Cramer, and he was from Odessa, Ukraine. His family had probably immigrated by ship in 1900 to flee the pogroms against the Jewish people. The family probably settled in Cincinnati, Ohio, where many Jews of that period lived. Aunt Ellie's birth father, who was then seventeen years old, somehow met Ruth Reese, who was of Welsh background and fifteen years old. The pregnancy resulted in my beautiful, intelligent Aunt Ellie. A single woman friend of the family had raised the baby until she was two and wished to adopt her, but the court ruled that a single woman could not adopt the child. The baby was then placed in a hospital, separated from the only mother she knew. She was unable to walk or talk, probably because of the sudden separation from the woman who had cared for her. Happily, a wise, compassionate doctor finally made a great match with Ellie and my loving grandparents.

Ned shared his father's passion for automobiles. In 1929 when Ned was twelve years old his dad bought a Pierce-Arrow Motor Car which was a status symbol owned by Hollywood stars and tycoons. The car was exceptionally long, with a 12-foot wheelbase and a V-8, the largest automobile engine in the world! The Pierce Arrow had moved the car's headlights from the traditional side placement by the radiator into flared housing molded into the front fenders of

The Pierce-Arrow Motor Car was extremely well designed and elegant and was irresistible to serious car enthusiasts like Will and Ned Prince

the car. It was fashionable and elegant, yet exceptionally well designed and extremely expensive. When Ned was not learning about car and engine design he loved to swim and play the piano. He was talented musically and could play almost any popular song of the day "by ear" meaning someone could sing him a tune and he would play it back on the piano without having to read the musical notes on paper. He attended University School, an all-boys private day school in the greater Cleveland area, graduating in 1936. Graduation from University School meant that he was automatically accepted at Cornell University. He joined the Psi Upsilon Fraternity and was a member of the Varsity Swim Team.

Ned's senior year of college was overshadowed by a World at War. On September 1, 1939, Germany invaded Poland and a few days later, Britain and France declared war on Germany followed by Australia, New Zealand, South Africa, and Canada. The United States took measures to assist the Western Allies and China whenever possible, but for the next two years the American public opposed any direct military intervention in the conflict.

One evening in his senior year of college, Ned drove himself home from a fraternity party and had a near fatal automobile accident which caused a compound fracture to his left leg. Because of this injury, he would not be eligible to enlist in the armed services should America

Ned Prince, 1936 (center) with his Psi U fraternity. His best friend, **William Baird**, is on his right.

enter the World War. He did recover from the accident and graduated in 1940 with a BS in Engineering. Ned then accepted the offer of an engineering position with Ingersoll-Rand and moved to Toledo, Ohio. Ellie graduated from Laurel School, an all-girl private school in northeast

Cleveland in 1941, and was accepted at Stanford University. Four months later, the Japanese bombed Pearl Harbor and America was at war.

Everyone in the United States who was able, organized to help with the war effort. People in every city were terrified that Germany or Japan would send airplanes to bomb them. Every major city prepared in case this would happen. At age 62, Will Prince volunteered to work on the civilian defense of Cleveland Heights and became a Senior Air Raid Warden. He personally delivered sandbags to fifty-one homes and trained his neighbors in the use of fire extinguishers and first aid. In June 1943 during an air raid drill, Will was shocked to notice that a neighbor had left a car parked in the street with the lights on. He ran out to the car to alert the owner when he suffered a serious heart attack and died several days later.

Will Prince loved to fish. Years after his death, his wife Helen said that this photo "looked so much like him."

Helen Prince was devastated at the loss of her husband. Her role in the household was limited to social obligations and caring for the children; she did not know how to drive a car, balance a checkbook, or pay bills. Ellie was forced to return home from Stanford to "run the house" for her mother. She eventually earned her B.A. degree from Case Western Reserve University and secured jobs as a script and commercial writer at several Cleveland radio stations. After her marriage and giving birth to two daughters, Ellie completed her master's degree in teaching and taught in the University Heights school system for 25 years, mostly as a very much in demand first grade teacher known for her creativity.

Eventually Helen became more independent. She moved to a lovely apartment in Shaker Heights, and I remember her as a kind and affectionate grandmother who served elegant meals with a full place setting of silverware, crystal, and china. After each course, she would ring a bell, and someone would come from the kitchen and clear the plates for the next course. She taught me how to knit, sew, and play cards. The memory I most cherish was when she would read me stories about Greek mythology. The fact that Helen's father was a professor of classical languages led her to share these tales with me. I absolutely loved these stories about gods, goddesses, and mythological creatures full of imagination, wonder and beauty.

Ellen Prince Rosendale with her family in 1968: husband King and daughters Ellen (named after her mother and great grandmother) and Avis.

On May 8, 1945, World War II in Europe ended. News of Germany's surrender reached the rest of the world and joyous crowds gathered to celebrate in the streets. On September 2, 1945, when victory was declared over Japan, the long and gruesome World War was finally over. People were devastated as they internalized the fact that so many friends and family were never coming home, but they were determined to get their lives back to normal as soon as possible.

The Danforth Family in 1944 (clockwise from top) Katherine Danforth Fisher with daughters Janie and Judy, Elizabeth Jane Danforth, John Hillyard Danforth, Arthur Edwards Danforth, Harold Coleman Danforth, William Howard Danforth, Marjorie Anne Danforth, and their mother, Jane Hillyard Danforth.

The Danforth family in Shaker Heights had committed six of their seven children to the war effort and miraculously all six were returning home: Captain William Danforth, a Marine Hell Diver Pilot; Marine Sargent Harold Danforth; Army Air Force Pfc. John Danforth; Navy Midshipman

Arthur Edwards Danforth, and twin girls Marjorie Anne and Elizabeth Jane Danforth who spent nine months in France as Red Cross Staff Assistants.

Elizabeth nicknamed "Betty," was a graduate of Lake Erie College majoring in philosophy and physical education. Her junior year of High School she was named the "prettiest girl at the Shaker High School's Junior May Prom." She said she caught the judges' attention because she was dancing with Clifford White, the school's star football player. She was an attractive young woman who was well known for her skill in riding horses and playing tennis and field hockey. (23) When she finished her tour in France at the end of World War II, she moved to Pittsburgh where she taught physical education at Chatham College for Women.

Elizabeth Danforth Prince as she left for her honeymoon at Sea Island, Georgia.

After the war, weddings dominated everyone's social calendar. Ned came home to Cleveland on weekends to attend the weddings of fraternity brothers and friends from high school. Betty also returned to Cleveland often to attend weddings for her brothers and friends. In the fall of 1947, Ned and Betty were seated at the same table for a friend's wedding dinner when it was discovered that the table was short one meal. Ned immediately proceeded to share his dinner with his mother who was seated next to him. Betty was impressed with the kind way Ned treated his mother and later, when he asked her for a date, she was happy to accept. Six months later, on March 13, 1948, they were married at Fairmont Presbyterian Church in Cleveland, and after a honeymoon at the Cloisters in Sea Island, Georgia, the couple resided in Toledo.

The following July, in 1949, the couple welcomed their first child, Edward Danforth Prince, followed in 1951 by a daughter, Marjorie Anne Prince and two years later, a son William Danforth Prince. Following Prince tradition, all three children were given family names.

Marjie, Danforth, and Ed in 1954 as their father recovered from polio at a hospital in Georgia

Later in 1953, Ned unexpectedly developed a case of the flu: sore throat, fever, tiredness, headache, and stiff neck. As his symptoms grew worse, Betty rushed him to the hospital and was told that he had contracted the polio virus. A young doctor examined Ned, came out to the Waiting Room, and told Betty, "I don't think he's going to make it." My mother was not sure how to proceed after hearing that comment; she had three children under the age of five and she was in Toledo, Ohio far from her family in Cleveland. Ned was put in an iron lung, a negative pressure chamber that assisted him with his breathing while his body fought the paralysis of the disease. He was then sent to an excellent treatment facility in Warm Springs, Georgia (one previously made famous by the polio-ridden U.S. president Franklin Delano Roosevelt,) where he began to make a full recovery. Two years later, Jonas Salk developed a polio vaccine, and the disease over the next six decades was virtually eradicated worldwide. After a year in Warm Springs, my father returned home to his family and his position as an engineer at Ingersoll-Rand. He had partial paralysis in his left arm, but for the rest of his life he never complained about the time he was critically ill. My mother attributed any strength of character she had later in life to the fact that she had managed her young family through this ordeal. It was a challenging experience for them both.

A fourth child, Helen Christie Prince, named after our grandmother, was born in 1956 and the family was now complete. Ingersoll-Rand moved the young household first to Chicago, Illinois and then to Easton, Pennsylvania. My mother pursued her love of teaching and for many years worked as the women's physical education instructor at Moravian Preparatory School in Bethlehem, Pennsylvania; then in 1980 she was honored to become the first woman Chairman of the Athletic Department at Moravian College.

As the family moved East closer to its original Dutch / English roots, our parents worked hard to instill in us many of the virtues celebrated by our ancestors. We were taught to be honest, truthful, and industrious. From an early age, my brothers had paper routes and once a week before school we all cleaned, vacuumed, and dusted the house. We were sent away to summer camp for eight weeks at a time to learn self-reliance and survival skills, and we regularly attended church as a family on Sundays. Education was given the highest priority; it was understood that we would all attend college and graduate. We were also taught by example to be public spirited and generous, volunteering to support causes that we believed were honorable. Most important of all, we were never discouraged if we made friends with children from a different race, religion, or ethnicity.

Four Princes in Easton, Pennsylvania 1968: Marjie, Ed, Christie, and Danforth

Chapter 11

Full Circle – Back to New York City and Brooklyn

After college graduation each of us left Pennsylvania to begin our lives and eventually we all relocated to within 500 miles of New York City. In 1980 my brother Bill moved to a grand old Victorian home (Magnolia House) on Staten Island. He inherited the large oil painting of Gertrude Martense Prince, and she found a place of honor, looking across New York's Upper Bay toward her former home in Flatbush.

Jordan and **Rachel Wolff** in Manhattan, 2008

In 2006 my son Jordan Danforth Wolff joined a Manhattan law firm and moved into an apartment on the lower East Side. My daughter, Rachel Helen Wolff relocated to New York a year later for employment and moved into an apartment on Park Avenue near Union Square. Both would make New York City their home for the next twelve years.

In time, Rachel married and her two children Zoe Rose Farley and James Brendan Farley, Jr were born at New York Presbyterian Weill Cornell Hospital which is located across the East River from the original farm "on the road to the ferry" next to the "Old Brooklyn Church" four miles north of the town of Flatbush. The original Dutch farmhouse was built in 1749 by Johannes De Bevoise and Hannah Betts. Now, thirteen generations later, the family has truly come "full circle," very close to its original point of origin in the Americas.

Acknowledgments

I want to thank my brother, William Danforth Prince, without whom this book would not have been possible. Thank you, Dan, for believing in this project from the very beginning and for giving me valuable insight every day. I also want to thank my husband, Donald Holt Troutman, and my children Jordan and Rachel for their love, kindness, and encouragement.

Also, central to the success of this book is Mary Martense of Flatbush, who married John Duffield Prince Jr in 1887 and who wrote a brief history *The Descendants of John Duffield Prince* for a Family Reunion in 1905. Her priceless information about the early origins of the family were invaluable to me.

Notes and Footnotes

(1) Actual typewritten account, *Something About the Edmistons* from around 1900 written for Edward Edmiston Mitchell, "Ned" born 1864 probably by his mother who ends the account by saying, "This is a crude little account, but may serve to straighten in your mind your family line on this side."

(2) Strong, Thomas Morris, *The History of the Town of Flatbush in Kings County Long Island*, p.11

(3) Ibid, p.29

(4) Ibid, p. 31

(5) Specifically, the house was bounded by Livingston, Hoyt, Nevins, and Fulton Streets

(6) Prince, Christopher, *The Autobiography of a Yankee Mariner*, p. 110

(7) In about 1802, Hezekiah Pierrepont (1768 – 1838) the famous landowner and developer in Brooklyn Heights bought **the original De Bevoise farm** (probably built around 1724 by Carel De Bevoise the County Judge, father of Johannes) in Brooklyn Heights plus three other farms in the area and built a mansion there.

(8) The cushion of the mahogany Chippendale Side Chair is stuffed with horsehair, a common practice in 1760.

(9) Susan Lawrence Prince, sister of John Duffield Prince, married William Rockwell in 1839. Mr. Rockwell was the District Attorney in Kings County from 1833 – 1839 and Judge of the New York State Supreme Court from 1853 until his death from yellow fever in 1856. Judge Rockwell is best known for the landmark streetcar desegregation case *Jennings vs. Third Avenue Railroad Company, 1854.* This case concerned a young free "Colored" woman, Elizabeth Jennings, who was thrown off a streetcar because the driver did not want "Colored Persons" to ride in his vehicle. When Miss Jennings brought a lawsuit against the railroad company, Judge William Rockwell instructed the all-white male jury that, "under the law, Colored persons, if sober, well behaved and free from disease, had the right to ride the streetcars and could neither be excluded by any rules of the Company, nor by force or violence." The jury found in favor Miss Jennings and awarded her $225 in damages. This case was important because it ultimately led to the racial desegregation of all public transportation in New York.

(10) The family name derived from the medieval French, **De Beauvoise,** and later simplified, probably in the New World, to **De Bevoise**. John Duffield De Bevoise Prince dropped this name "for convenience" later in life.

(11) Vanderbilt, Gertrude Lefferts, *The Social History of Flatbush*, p. 350

(12) Ibid, p. 249 - 251

(13) Strong, Op-Cit, p. 51

(14) Vanderbilt, Op-Cit, p. 222

(15) Ibid, p. 173

(16) Ibid, p. 222

(17) Ibid, p. 214

(18) Briefly, Harriet Beecher Stowe is our second cousin, four generations removed: Harriet Beecher Stowe's grandfather, David Beecher (1738 – 1805) married Ester Lyman whose father Ebenezer Lyman was killed in a fire at age 44 (1709 – 1753). He was born in Northampton, MA. He is our fifth great

grandfather and thus our common ancestor with Harriet. Ester Lyman's niece, Hannah, married the Reverend Alvan Hyde Ingersoll whose son, Jonathan Edwards Ingersoll was the father of our great grandmother Kate Cornelia Ingersoll, mother of Arthur Edwards Danforth

(19)   My father told me that William Babcock was instrumental in manufacturing an extremely deadly rifle that was used in the Civil War. As a young girl I did not really understand what this meant, but later in life I understood that in war an army needs weapons, but I was dismayed that my great uncle was the person who was responsible for making a rifle which was more efficient and deadly.

(20)   *The Cleveland Plain Dealer*, June 2, 1943

(21)   Mary Margaret Mitchell was the great great granddaughter of "The Lady" and Mr. Galbraith, who are mentioned in the story which opens this book. Mary's brother was Edward Edmiston Mitchell, "Ned", the young man for whom the story was originally written.

(22)   Some of the art Ellen Babcock Prince acquired on her travels later in life are still in the family today: an art nouveau bronze statue by a French sculptor E. Picault, a gilded Coromandel mirror from Gumps in San Francisco, and an award-winning American painting "Florida Dunes," inspired by Claude Monet.

(23)   I mentioned that Betty Danforth was "skilled in riding horses and playing tennis and field hockey" but these words do not say enough. Betty was extremely competent in these sports. As a young woman, she was a judge at horse shows in the Cleveland area because she was a very good English style rider. In tennis, she knew several Wimbledon champions and played tennis with them on a regular basis, including Dorothy Round who won the Wimbledon Woman's singles title in 1934 and 1937. In field hockey she was a member of the Great Lakes Field Hockey Team in the late 1930's and was a referee as well as a coach in the sport.

Bibliography

McCullough, David, *1776*, Simon & Schuster, New York, 2005

Prince, Christopher, *The Autobiography of a Yankee Mariner*, Brassey, Inc, Dulles, Virginia, 2002

Rutherfurd, Edward, *New York*, Random House, New York, 2009

Strong, Thomas Morris, *The History of the Town of Flatbush in Kings County Long Island*, Thomas Mercein, Jr. New York, 1842

Vanderbilt, Gertrude Lefferts, *The Social History of Flatbush*, D. Appleton and Company, New York, 1899

The Prince Family

Elder John Prince 1610/1637/1676
Arrived in Boston 1633
Married Alice Honor 1637; son Thomas

Captain Thomas Prince 1658/1686/1704
Sailed Ship *Dolphin* out of Boston for 19 Years
Married Ruth Turner; son Job

Captain Job Prince 1695/1719/1734
Married Abigail Kimball in 1719
Both died in 1734 leaving young son Christopher aged 3

Colonel Christopher Prince 1730/1757/1799
Became a partner in *Prince Brothers*, Boston - family trading company
Married Mary Foster 1757; son John
Moved to Digby, Nova Scotia in 1760
After death of Mary, married Anna Payson 1787

John Prince 1760/1782/
Born in Boston, taken to Nova Scotia as an infant
Married Sarah Willoughby; son Christopher
Details of death unknown "disappeared in Canada"

Captain Christopher Prince 1784/1808/
Born in Nova Scotia; moved to New York City with Uncle Benjamin Prince
Sailed Ship *Rebecca* out of New York for 12 years
Married Anna Duffield; six children
Buried at sea, details unknown

John Duffield Prince 1814/1835/1888
Founder of *John D. Prince and Sons*
Married Gertrude Helen Martense in 1835; 10 children

Jacob Van Brunt Prince 1844/1877/1913
Married Ellen Harriet Babcock in 1877; only child, William Babcock

William Babcock Prince 1879/1913/1943
Relocated to Cleveland in 1900 after college graduation
Director of Bishop and Babcock Company, President of *Prince & Izant Company*
Married Helen Christie in 1913; son Edward Mitchell "Ned", daughter Ellen Babcock

Edward Mitchell Prince 1917/1948/2001
Married Elizabeth Jane Danforth in 1948; four children
Relocated to Toledo, Ohio; Hinsdale, Illinois; Easton, Pennsylvania

Edward Danforth Prince, 1949
Married Caroline Elizabeth Pittman in 1974
Parents to Elizabeth Ann Prince

Marjorie Anne Prince, 1951
Married Mark Steven Wolff in 1975
Parents to Jordan Danforth Wolff and Rachel Helen Wolff
Married Donald Holt Troutman in 2004

William Danforth Prince, 1953
Founder and President of Blood Moon Productions *(www.BloodMoonProductions.com)*
Business Partner and Long Time Companion of Darwin Porter

Helen Christie Prince, 1956
Married Richard Kevin Barry in 1980
Parents to Meghan Elizabeth Barry and Colin Hillyard Barry

Marjorie Anne Prince

A native of Bethlehem, Pennsylvania and a graduate of William Smith College with a B.A. in English and Education and a minor in History, Marjie taught high school English at the American Schools in Mexico City and Monterrey before moving Longview, Texas where she taught English As A Second Language at the University of Texas at Tyler. In 1987 she moved with her young family to Pittsburgh, Pennsylvania and completed studies in Human Resources Management at the University of Pittsburgh. For over thirty years she has lived in North Carolina and worked in the field of Human Resources as a Manager, a Director, and a consultant. She is a passionate reader of history, fiction and nonfiction and takes great pride in her roles as mother, grandmother, wife, sister, friend, golfer, bird watcher and gardener.